Down to Earth
Youth Study Book

DOWN TO EARTH:
The Hopes & Fears of All the Years
Are Met in Thee Tonight

Down to Earth

978-1-5018-2339-8

978-1-5018-2340-4 eBook

978-1-5018-2341-1 Large Print

Down to Earth: Devotions for the Season

978-1-5018-2344-2

978-1-5018-2345-9 eBook

Down to Earth: DVD

978-1-5018-2346-6

Down to Earth: Leader Guide

978-1-5018-2342-8

978-1-5018-2343-5 eBook

Down to Earth: Youth Study Book

978-1-5018-2352-7

978-1-5018-2353-4 eBook

Down to Earth: Children's Leader Guide

978-1-5018-2354-1

Also by Mike Slaughter

Change the World

Christmas Is Not Your Birthday

Dare to Dream

Hijacked

Momentum for Life

Money Matters

Real Followers

Renegade Gospel

shiny gods

Spiritual Entrepreneurs

The Christian Wallet

The Passionate Church

UnLearning Church

Upside Living in a
   Downside Economy

For more information, visit www.MikeSlaughter.com.

Mike
Slaughter

The
Hopes & Fears
of All the Years

Down
TO
Earth

Are Met in
Thee
Tonight

With
Rachel Billups

Youth Study Book
by Kevin Alton

Abingdon Press / Nashville

Down to Earth
Youth Study Book

16 17 18 19 20 21 22 23 24 25 — 10 9 8 7 6 5 4 3 2 1
MANUFACTURED IN THE UNITED STATES OF AMERICA

CONTENTS

INTRODUCTION

Sometimes Advent feels like we're hitting the reset button.

I ride a motorcycle as my primary transportation. You may not realize it, but a lot of motorcycles—especially older ones—don't have gas gauges. You keep track of how far you've traveled on your current tank of gas by using the odometer. Most tanks have a small reserve at the bottom; you can ride with your fuel switch set on "main" and let the bike sputtering let you know when to switch to reserve, then get thyself to a gas station. Others play fast and loose and keep it set on reserve—no warning that you're almost out.

So a critical function of riding my motorcycle is resetting the odometer to zero whenever I stop for gas. Zeroing out tells me where I am in my journey—how far I've come, how far I've got to go. If I forget to reset, I'm sure to be a little confused not far down the road.

I like to think of Advent like that. It's a chance to reset, regroup, get my bearings, and just breathe for a minute before launching back out into the journey.

One of the great joys of riding a motorcycle is the connection with the world around you, and that's very much where we're headed with this

Advent series. We're going to be exploring down-to-earth living, as we remember and rejoice in the coming down-to-earth incarnation of God among us.

I hope that you'll enjoy this journey with me through down-to-earth love, humility, lifestyle, and obedience, and that you'll find yourselves closer to God and each other as Christmas approaches.

To the Leader

This book can be read by individual youth during the Advent and Christmas season, and it can also be used very effectively in a group. The book's format is designed so that group activities will flow naturally in the following categories.

Reading and Reflecting

Each chapter begins with a section exploring a theme and Scripture, with examples from my own family and ministry experiences.

Going Deeper

Here you'll find more devotional thoughts, using Scripture that complements the main text for the chapter. If you're using this book with a group, a helpful approach is to have group members commit to completing the reading and devotionals before coming together as a group.

Making It Personal

These are some reflective thoughts and questions that look back over the texts and themes and are intended to be answered alone. If you've completed the devotions during the week, it might be helpful to look over this section right before you go to meet with your group. If you're not meeting with a group, you can use them whenever you like.

Sharing Thoughts and Feelings

These group questions can serve as an icebreaker to open your group time together. They should also allow anyone who hasn't read the chapter in the book to be drawn in to the conversation.

Doing Things Together

Each chapter concludes with two fifteen-minute activities designed to engage your group with the material in a new way. Supplies are minimal, but be sure that someone is in charge of bringing anything necessary to the experience. Most of the activities wrap up with one or two additional discussion questions or a peek back at the text.

Listening for God

Chapters end with a prayer. You and the group members can use the prayer as is or substitute a prayer of your own.

Blessings to you on your journey through Advent!

1.
Down to Earth
Love

1.

DOWN TO EARTH LOVE

Therefore, if there is any encouragement in Christ, any comfort in love, any sharing in the Spirit, any sympathy, complete my joy by thinking the same way, having the same love, being united, and agreeing with each other. Don't do anything for selfish purposes, but with humility think of others as better than yourselves. Instead of each person watching out for their own good, watch out for what is better for others. (Philippians 2:1-4)

Reading and Reflecting

Love Beyond Reason

It started when my wife and I decided to hang out in Chattanooga one Saturday afternoon.

We live near Chattanooga and have always loved the downtown area, even when it had been a little rundown during our college years. These days it has experienced a thriving rebirth. It's packed with great places to eat and a beautiful, family-friendly waterfront area on both banks of the Tennessee River. That day we'd brought a picnic lunch, and when it was time to eat we sought shelter from the sun in an outdoor amphitheater beneath the Walnut Street walking bridge. We'd made too many sandwiches, as it turned out, and while we were eating we'd noticed a man sleeping near the back of the amphitheater, surrounded by a small collection of personal belongings. We were unsure about waking him but finally decided to risk disturbing him to offer him some food.

In the resulting conversation, we found that this man was living in Chattanooga temporarily, without permanent lodging. He was sleeping under bridges, occasionally moving as he was noticed by police or for his own sense of security. I was wary of his story as he started to relate it, having heard many dubious accounts of life circumstances when I was working in downtown Atlanta.

What made his story stand out from others I'd heard was his self-reliance. He didn't ask for more than we were offering. He didn't want money. He had a *plan*. He was from Florida, where he lived and worked as a carpenter. Times were tough; the housing market had collapsed and work was slow. He'd driven to Chattanooga for a job prospect that didn't work out. As he was leaving to head back to Florida, his truck had broken down on the Interstate. He left the highway to get some lunch and sort out his options. When he returned, his truck had already been towed. Boom—homeless, in the space of one afternoon.

The man didn't have friends or relations anywhere close by; his only family was an estranged sister out in California. And even if he could have figured out where the truck had been towed, it wouldn't have been worth recovering because it wasn't in working order.

In the time between that day and our meeting him, he had managed to find a temporary job that promised to last a few months. He was picked up at a certain intersection each day. He had figured out that if he could make it through the next ten days or so under the bridge, he would have saved enough to move to a local extended-stay motel. There he could more comfortably work out the remaining weeks of the job, and by the time it was over he'd have enough money to get back to Florida a little ahead on his rent to look for work down there.

Listening to him, I was haunted by the fragility of what I thought of as normal life. I mean, I knew in theory that much of what we consider to be our day-to-day reality could be upended. But to have it all go away so quickly...

I decided I wanted to experience something like what the man had gone through. So I decided to do it for Lent.

An Advent Study?

Yes, you're reading the right book; it's for Advent, not Lent. We'll get to that shortly. Advent is all about expectation and waiting, isn't it? So stay with me.

My Lenten practice was this: I would live in just one set of clothing for the duration of the season. I couldn't use the ordinary means of cleaning my clothing or my body; all I allowed myself was fifteen minutes every other day to get as much of me or my clothing cleaned as possible in a bathroom sink with hand soap, figuring that was about how long a person could be in a gas station bathroom before being run off. I wouldn't be able to shave. It was going to get icky.

The experience genuinely changed me as a person, but that experience is a story for another day. The real story here is how I discovered the depth of down-to-earth love that existed in my life.

You see, as unpleasant as I might have been during Lent for the people at church and elsewhere in my life, they would only have to put up with me for a few hours a week. Sure, they would shake their heads, and some of them might wonder if the youth minister had lost his marbles. (Interestingly, unless my condition was pointed out to them, the youth group completely forgot I was doing it.) But the church members and the youth group weren't the issue; the issue was Britta, my wife.

Britta had to see me every day. Britta had to live with a husband who, after the first week, could really only hope to achieve "not as gross and smelly." But she stood by me through it all. A leadership team I was working with at the time dubbed her "St. Britta." The adults at church would joke, "How is Britta's Lenten thing going?" to point out that I'd inadvertently designed a collateral Lenten sacrifice for her.

Loving Through the Grit

It may have amounted to an unintended Lenten sacrifice for Britta, but you wouldn't have known it. She bore with me through it all. Not once did she object to how I looked. Or smelled. There were experiences that season that had us cracking up and others that had us in tears. She encouraged me to find grace within the experience.

It was an unexpected reminder of the depth of Britta's love for me, beyond all that you'd ever ask of anyone.

I knew, of course, that I wouldn't really be replicating the experience of the guy from the amphitheater. I got to pick the clothes I was abandoned in. I got to sleep in my own real bed in my own real house. I got to sit in an air-conditioned office every day. But the transforming part was realizing that my clearest advantage was the ability to be *loved* through the experience.

The love Britta showed me was, and is, reminiscent of the love Jesus would bring to the world as he came. It was the love we're told to emulate in today's Scripture: "Don't do anything for selfish purposes, but with humility think of others as better than yourselves. Instead of each person watching out for their own good, watch out for what is better for others" (Philippians 2:3-4).

It should be the simplest thing, but every year at Advent we end up reminding ourselves of the same thing: Christ came down to earth. Christ showed us a revolutionary way to love and live and showed us that it was *possible* to live and love like that.

All we have to do is follow.

Going Deeper

Teacher's Pet

Peter was an exuberant disciple. He wanted so badly to get it right. His was probably the first hand raised every time Jesus asked a question: "Oh, me, me, me. Pick me!" For an example, read Matthew 18:21-33, the parable of the unforgiving servant.

Peter had started in the right direction but hadn't figured out how to get there. Forgiveness wasn't how Jewish society was ordered. Their practice of faith—which would have been the practice of these fishermen-turned-disciples—was steeped in laws and rules for all areas of life. Violation of the laws and rules had clear consequences. Forgiveness would indicate a departure from those rules into a whole new kind of thinking.

In making that step Peter was on the right track; he realized that forgiveness is a desirable thing in a new kind of kingdom. But Peter wanted rules attached to it! "I'll forgive them," he might have said, "because Jesus told me to. But how many times?"

The kind of forgiveness that Jesus taught wasn't rules-oriented or metered by any sense of fairness. A down-to-earth love sets all that structure aside. It's just you and me, and I forgive you. Period.

For reflection:

- When have you had to overcome the desire to *stop* forgiving someone? Do you want your forgiveness to be rooted in fairness or in love?
- What do you think Peter learned from the parable of the unforgiving servant?
- How does our ability to forgive others demonstrate our understanding of how we have been forgiven?

Recipe for Love

Love can stand alone, but it can also be a by-product of other attitudes and behaviors. Stand-alone love can be very conditional. I love people who love me. I love friends who don't hurt my feelings. I love people with whom I have things in common. But if we are to experience the kind of down-to-earth love that Jesus came to demonstrate, we have to move beyond conditional love into unconditional love. And there are behaviors associated with it.

Check out Paul's comments about it in Ephesians 4:1-3. He doesn't jump right in to telling us to love each other. He begins by saying to "conduct yourselves with all humility, gentleness, and patience" (v. 3). Those are some of the ingredients that make up love. If you leave the house every morning determined to be humble, gentle, and patient, it doesn't matter what anybody confronts you with. Your attitude is humility, gentleness, and patience. And guess what? For those you encounter, it will add up to love.

For reflection:

- When do you struggle most to be a loving person? Is it when you're tired? when people are snarky toward you? What puts you over the edge?
- What are some opportunities you've passed up recently to show humility, gentleness, and patience?
- What are some of the ways you've been loved that have helped you learn better habits for loving others?

The Love Chapter

Read 1 Corinthians 13. Yup, the whole chapter.

This is one of the most famous passages from the Bible, if fame can be ascribed to words. It gets trotted out at a lot of weddings, as I suppose it should. I especially like the way it starts. (Pardon the loose translation, written by me.)

Even if I fluently speak the most elegant, poetic languages on earth or the mysterious and otherworldly tongues of angels—

if I don't have love, I'm really like crash, bash, ting-tang smash. Without love, I'm a completely disordered disaster. If I do all manner of crazy cool things but don't have love, I'm nothing. Nothing! (1 Corinthians 13:1-2 , my translation))

That should give us a little perspective on the priority we should give to loving. We want to love but don't ever seem to get there. We tightly grasp our love in both hands, barely letting it slip out to a select few—and even then, usually with conditions. How can we get over ourselves?

For reflection:

- I know it's not easy. We're geared to be defensive; love, at its heart, lets down its guard and is completely defenseless. What keeps you from letting down your guard with those who are closest to you? Who do you trust with your deepest hurts?
- How does your trust of others match up with others' trust in you? How have you respected others when they've been vulnerable to you?
- Have you ever been hurt when you allowed yourself to be vulnerable?
- What do you think about the complete vulnerability that's called by the love described in 1 Corinthians 13?

Making It Personal

The kind of down-to-earth love we're talking about is significant because it's the very love that infuses our lives at Advent. Keep in mind that it's different from Christmas card love or romantic love—this love is grittier than that. This is the kind of love that fights through all the junk that life flings at us. This is the kind of love that cares for us when we're sick. It surrounds us when we've failed. This kind of love can even survive a cheap shot when we're hurt or angry.

19

- It's critical for us as Christians to embrace this kind of down-to-earth love, because *so many* people won't get to experience that love if we don't bring it to them. A happy home life is not only no longer a guarantee; it's nearly out of the norm. Life, even in America, isn't lived in equity. People are defensive. On guard. Afraid. So in need of love.

But we can't reach out with a false attempt at down-to-earth love. People will see right through us if we're faking it or offering a shallow, conditional version of Jesus' love.

Take a good hard look at how you've experienced love in this world. Has your life equipped you to love others or conditioned you to insulate yourself? What fears or reservations do you have about offering God's love to those around you? Are there people you need to forgive before you can move to a place of love?

If you've been hurt by people who should have been caring for you, consider reaching out for help. Your school has staff dedicated to your personal well-being, and trusted adults at church can guide you to care that can begin to restore you.

Sharing Thoughts and Feelings

Spend some time with a group discussing these questions:

- When you hear the phrase *down to earth*, what does it mean to you?
- What about the phrase *down-to-earth love*? How is it different from other definitions of love that you've heard or experienced?
- If you were going to "love like Jesus," what would have to change? Are you more inclined to think of others first, or yourself? Why is that? When have you been surprised to receive God's love from another person?

- When or how have you seen people not loved by other Christians? What were the circumstances? How did that experience affect those people's image of the church or of God?
- When have you had to be transparent about your own struggle to emulate the love of God? How might it help others to hear of your struggles, even as you're helping them?

Doing Things Together

Love, Love Me Don't

Supplies: Posterboard and markers

Sometimes the best way to enact change in our lives is to be completely honest about where we are. Take a sheet of posterboard and write out the "Love is" statements from 1 Corinthians 13, beginning with "Love is patient" in verse 4 and continuing through "Love never fails" in verse 8. Write each statement on a single line. When you have them all written out, cut the phrases apart and jumble them together, face down, on the floor.

- Before you begin, tell the group this is an exercise of *trust*; if anyone is unwilling to participate or respect what the others in the group may share, this is a good time to step out for a few minutes.
- Choose someone to start. That person will pick up one of the strips of posterboard, read aloud the "Love is" statement on it, and then share a time when they did the *opposite*. If people are embarrassed or hesitant to do this, remind them that we're all capable of mangling our intentions to love others as Christ loves us; this activity is meant to help generate some conversation about how we can avoid those missteps.

- After the first person shares, have the person choose who goes next. Continue reading and sharing until all of the strips have been read or until everyone has shared, whichever comes last. Afterward, debrief using the following questions:
  o How difficult was it to be honest about times when we have gotten love wrong? What makes that difficult?
  o Does anyone here think they've already achieved the ability to love just like Jesus? If not, why is it so hard to admit that we struggle with this?

Put the strips back on the floor, face down, and reshuffle them. Go through the exercise again, and this time when you pick up a strip, share a time where you got that one right. Same rules; keep going until everyone has gone and all of the strips have been used. Now ask:

- Did this version of the activity feel better? Why or why not?
- What are some ways we can help others celebrate when we see them getting it right?

Spin the Bottle

Supplies: A full twenty-ounce beverage bottle

Here's a variation on Spin the Bottle that should be fun, constructive, and kiss-free.

Sit in a circle with the bottle in the middle, and spin the bottle. Whoever it points to should tell the group one thing that makes them feel down-to-earth loved every time it happens. Use this phrase: "I love it when _____." It could be coming home to find out your bed has been made or that someone has hung clean clothes in your closet. It could be when you make eye contact with a buddy you sit with on the school bus. It's totally up to you what you say, but make sure it's sincere and also that we're respecting others as they share.

Spin again and again, until everyone has had a chance to go. Then close with these questions:

- What feels good about remembering things that make you feel loved?
- What keeps us from making other people feel like that all the time?
- What's one way you're looking forward to feeling loved during Advent this year?
- Who is going to tell their parents we played Spin the Bottle without explaining how we did it differently?

Listening for God

God, thank you for sending Jesus to show us your down-to-earth love. Help us to follow his example in the ways that we treat others and ourselves. Amen!

2.
Down to Earth
Humility

2.

DOWN TO EARTH HUMILITY

Adopt the attitude that was in Christ Jesus:

> *Though he was in the form of God,*
> *he did not consider being equal with God*
> *something to exploit.*
> *But he emptied himself*
> *by taking the form of a slave*
> *and by becoming like human beings.*
> *When he found himself in the form of a human,*
> *he humbled himself by becoming obedient to the*
> *point of death,*
> *even death on a cross.*

> *(Philippians 2:5-8)*

Reading and Reflecting

The Best

No one is listening to anyone. That's where we've arrived.

With the advent of social media (see what I did there?) and online interaction, a key component to civil dialogue was removed: having to say anything directly to another person's face. When you say something directly to someone else, you cannot avoid taking their feelings into account. You're going to have to see with your own eyes how your words affect them. You'll have to deal with their body language and whether you've hurt them or made them happy. Being in the presence of the other person tempers your statements. We're not inclined to be as aggressive with our opinion in person, because we know the other person is going to have a chance to react in real time, and we're going to have to deal with that response.

Talking in person, in general, makes us better people.

Unfortunately, we've learned that we don't actually have to talk to people. If we don't have to talk to them, we don't have to listen to them. The less we hear from them, the less we know about them. The less we know about them—and here's the dangerous turn—the more we start to *fear* them. Ignorance is hardly bliss.

What makes that dangerous? At the middle school and high school level, it mostly turns into an ugly clique system, with various groups jostling for social position. At the community level, it turns into those with power leveraging it over those without power.

Humility

If, rather than power, our communities were rooted in humility—putting the other person first—then equity and equality wouldn't be a social issue. Racism wouldn't exist. The economic gap between the rich and poor would close.

But we're *not* rooted in humility. So we've become rooted in fear. And what do we do when we're afraid? We get defensive.

Check your social media feed. A large percentage of it is people lashing out at each other. *Any* social issue raised is met with a barrage of knee-jerk criticism. As I write this, debate is raging over public restrooms—specifically, whether transgendered people can use the restroom of the gender they identify as, or if those people must use the bathroom that corresponds to the gender on their birth certificates. It's a complicated issue, to be sure. Having always held the opinion that I don't want to be in the bathroom with *anybody*, I understand the concerns coming from all sides. What I'm not hearing often enough, though, is anyone discussing it as if there are *real people* involved.

If you don't acknowledge real people, you don't have to listen. If you don't have to listen—and if you have power—then you get to tell other people how things are going to be.

Power Converter

This is why Jesus' kingdom was—and remains—so radical. It doesn't bring an end to power; it changes what power is and what it means to have power. In Jesus' kingdom, power is the ability to build the road to equity. In Jesus' kingdom, *having* power means having the responsibility to make sure that power is used wisely. How do we get there?

We begin with down-to-earth humility.

- Jesus showed us how. "Though he was in the form of God, / he did not consider being equal with God something to exploit" (Philippians 2:6). Jesus had ultimate power but made himself less and less, *humbling* himself to the point of death on a cross.
- Did you notice what Jesus *didn't* do? He didn't set power aside. He could have; he had the option of just putting it away and living an ordinary life. Fully human. Totally a viable option. Yet Jesus stayed in it, choosing instead to demonstrate *how* to live

29

with power when you have it. You use it to put others first. You use it to demonstrate love to everyone you meet. You use it to listen. You use it to *hear*, which isn't always the same thing. You use it to practice humility. And the more power you get, the more chances you have to practice.

At the heart of things, not a lot has changed since Jesus came. We see the same broken, ugly version of abuse from those in power. When we're the ones with power, we mostly use it to promote ourselves and hold others back. Sometimes we don't even do it intentionally; it's just that we were raised in a place of privilege and simply don't see the advantages we have over others. But if we can take it a step at a time and begin practicing God's down-to-earth humility, slowly but surely we'll usher in the upside-down kingdom of God.

Going Deeper

Better Than You

We can be so wrapped up in our own existence that we're unaware of how our lives affect the people around us. That's one kind of not living in humility. Other kinds can be far more toxic—like *being* aware of how our lives affect the people around us and not caring. Or seeing the inequity between our life and someone else's life and accepting it. Nothing about these attitudes resemble Christlike living, and yet we touch on these attitudes all the time. For example, have you ever expressed gratitude that your life isn't like someone else's? Have you ever referenced the "blessings" in your life in comparison to someone with less?

Read Luke 18:9-14.

- I can't tell you how many mission trips I've been on with youth in which someone—adults included—said, "It just makes you so grateful for what you have." *Every time* that was expressed, it was stated sincerely, but what does it say about us when our main point of interaction with someone's life is to be grateful we're not living it? How can we move through life *allowing* others to exist in lives we couldn't bear to live ourselves?

The Pharisees catch a lot of grief from Christians—we love to paint them as the "bad guys" in Scripture. But doesn't the Pharisee in Jesus' story sound an awful lot like us when we're on a mission trip? The Pharisee says, "God, I thank you that I'm not like everyone else." We say, "Thank you God, that I don't live in a place like this."

We can't improve the lives of everyone, but are we even trying?

For reflection:

- Have you ever thought or prayed like that?
- Can you think of ways to be grateful for what you have without comparing it to what someone else has?

Kids Are the Best

The disciples would have had a hard time choosing teams for kickball.

You know the drill: athleticism and popularity are quickly assessed, and everybody from the middle of the pack down goes home discouraged. I don't think the disciples could have handled the pressure. They all wanted to be first. They were following Jesus partly because they had some notion of a kingdom that he was trying to establish, and they were certainly interested in overthrowing the one that they currently lived under. But their perpetual interest was in who among them was the greatest, which showed they had *no* notion of the kind of humility that would be required to succeed in launching the kingdom of heaven.

Read Matthew 18:1-5.

As you can see from this story, when the disciples asked who was the greatest, Jesus surprised them by saying, "Kids are the greatest." He wasn't trying to be cute or have a heartwarming children's moment right before the offering and choral anthem. Jesus was saying to take whatever you were thinking about power, rank, and privilege and reverse it. Turn it inside out. Upside down.

Take a look at Jesus' answer, as expressed in the NRSV: "Truly I tell you, unless you change and become like children, you will never enter the kingdom of heaven." (v. 3).

Yikes.

For reflection:

- We have the benefit of a lot of history to put Jesus' words in context. Do you think you would you have been any different from the disciples in wanting to be the greatest?
- What are some examples of when you've worried about where you ranked against others?
- When have you been jealous of things in other people's lives? How can down-to-earth humility help improve that in the future?

No Seriously, Who's the Best?

If you didn't believe me about the disciples' fixation on power-ranking themselves on a scale from 1 to 12, check out Mark 9:30-37.

To sum up the story, Jesus says (roughly), "I'm gonna die." To which the disciples respond by debating which of them is the best. Jesus says (not really), "I feel so *heard*."

You could argue, in the disciples' defense, that they didn't understand what Jesus meant and were afraid to ask him. After all, that is what it says in verse 32. Here, though, Jesus is like the parent driving the minivan on vacation. He interrupts an argument to give some instructions for when they arrive: "Everybody stay in the car until I get us checked in." The kids stare blankly, and then go back to fighting.

Jesus, probably more patient than the parent driving the minivan, calls for a little sit-down with the disciples, saying, "Whoever wants to be first must be least of all and the servant of all" (v. 35).

The disciples never really get it, at least while Jesus is with them. Even as he's leaving them in Acts, they're still asking if *now* is when he's going to restore the kingdom of Israel. When he ascends, maybe it's just to keep them from asking one last time who is the best.

For reflection:

- How much do you let your self-worth ride on where you think you rank among the people you know?
- Have you ever let your comparison with other people affect how you treat them—or yourself?

Making It Personal

You've probably encountered a social issue where you are genuinely bothered by the ugly way it's being handled online or in the media. The news prefers to fixate on anything that gets people riled up, and it's become nearly impossible to find a source of information that is anywhere near neutral in its presentation. We live in the information age, and we've gotten so good at it that you can even filter what news gets to you!

It's difficult to know where to jump in to help anyone. It seems like *everyone* has some cause they want you to support, and it's difficult to fight through the sheer volume of information to get any clarity on the things you do care about.

Humility can seem like a weak first step in the right direction, but Jesus has assured us by his very example that it's the best one. There will be challenges, and it will be difficult. Nearly every one of Jesus' first disciples died for following Jesus—that can be an intimidating reality to consider. Remember though, we're not called to *win*. We're called to follow. We're called to real, genuine, down-to-earth humility.

Often we have very specific, unnamed issues that hold us back from laying our own will aside in order to serve God humbly. Do you know what your issues are? What things in your life do you want to gain control of or to keep control over?

Sharing Thoughts and Feelings

Spend some time with a group discussing these questions:

- Before you read this chapter, how would you have described "down-to-earth humility"? Is humility something you try to exercise? If so, how and when do you do it?

- What social issues have you observed being argued about online and in your social media feed?

- When have you been overwhelmed by all the noise surrounding social issues? How do you sort through it all?

- What is one real way you can put others before yourself without it looking like grandstanding?

- When have you had someone compare themselves with you in a negative way? Did they do it to your face or behind your back? When have you compared someone with you in a negative way? How do you leave that kind of behavior behind?

Doing Things Together

Hashtag

Supplies: Blank paper and pens

- The *humblebrag* emerged online pretty quickly when Facebook opened up from a college-only social network to go wide with the public. Quietly patting yourself on the back isn't a new thing, but online and social media tools gave us an opportunity to "quietly" mention our awesomeness to a much wider audience.
- "Feeling #blessed to relax in the backyard with a few close friends by the Olympic-sized swimming pool." That may be an over-the-top example, but you get the idea. Another popular form of humblebrag is casually name-dropping minor (or major!) celebrities. One of the most tempting forms is to retweet the tweet of someone's retweet of *you*—it screams, "Look! I'm popular!" but in a super-casual way. Like it was NBD.

Have you ever heard someone humblebrag about doing good in the world? This one does the trick nicely: "Totally exhausted from serving in the soup kitchen this A.M." Here's one you might see following a mission trip: "Feeling great about changing lives today in Haiti."

Spend a few minutes coming up with some mission-oriented humblebrags of your own. Work individually and then, if you're with a group, come together to compare. For bonus points, draw out the post the way it might actually appear on a social network. (Minus 100 points for actually posting any of these.) Try to come up with at least three humblebrags each.

After you've had some time to work, come back together to share what you created. When all the posts have been read out loud, take a couple of minutes to put them in order from humblebrag to humblebraggest. Wrap up with these questions:

- Are any of these humblebrags ones you've actually seen online or in social media?
- How would you respond if you did see one of these in your feed? Would you respond in reality or just in your head?
- What does a humblebrag have to do with actual humility? How can we move from trumpeting the good we're doing to a place of genuine humility?

Behind the Behind-the-Scenes

Supplies: Enough chairs for everyone, a source of music

Play a game of musical chairs. The basic rules are as follows:

- Begin with everyone seated. Music is played; while it's playing, one chair is removed as everyone stands and begins to circle the available chairs. At some point the music is stopped, and everyone tries to land in one of the chairs. Since one chair is missing, somebody is *out*. Repeat until you're down to one chair and two players.

If your group is meeting in a home and the seats are too cumbersome to remove, you can instead simply designate them as off-limits one at a time as the game is played.

- When you've played down to a single winner, play a *reverse* game of musical chairs. The winner can choose someone to reenter the game by saying, "[Someone's name], would you like to join me?" They reply, "Of course!" and reenter.

- It's still just the two of them with the one chair, however. So this time when the music stops, whoever gets the chair *immediately* stands back up saying, "Oh, I'm sorry, let me get you a chair," and proceeds to do so (or points out an off-limits chair that is now back in play). The person who was just called back in now invites someone else into the game: "[Someone's name], would you like to join us?"

Repeat this process until everyone has a seat again. Wrap up with these questions:

- Sometimes when we're serving others, it's tempting to look out for our own interests first—like fighting to get a chair and then offering to serve the person you just outplayed. Or humblebragging from a mission trip. What are some ways we can intentionally put others first while we're putting others first?
- In other words, how can we make sure we're doing mission work with real humility? How can we put those people before us while we're also serving them?

Listening for God

God, Jesus was the ultimate example of down-to-earth humility. Help us to carry that humility in our hearts as we engage the many needs of our neighbors. Amen!

3.
Down to Earth
Lifestyle

3.

DOWN TO EARTH LIFESTYLE

This is how the birth of Jesus Christ took place. When Mary his mother was engaged to Joseph, before they were married, she became pregnant by the Holy Spirit. Joseph her husband was a righteous man. Because he didn't want to humiliate her, he decided to call off their engagement quietly. As he was thinking about this, an angel from the Lord appeared to him in a dream and said, "Joseph son of David, don't be afraid to take Mary as your wife..." When Joseph woke up, he did just as an angel from God commanded and took Mary as his wife.
(Matthew 1:18-20, 24)

Reading and Reflecting

Medicine Is the Best Medicine

I let way too much time pass before I admitted there was something critically wrong with my back.

It wasn't out of bravado or anything. I just hate going to the doctor. I have a particularly high level of medical anxiety. If one of our kids bleeds or gets sick, my wife deals with it so that she's not suddenly presented with two patients instead of one.

The best we can guess, my back injury began when I was just out of high school, working at an office supply retailer. I was at the front of the store, waiting to assist a customer to the car with a new office desk. For those of you who aren't familiar with unassembled office furniture, the important thing to know is that it involves a feat of physics, fitting a desk that will fill half a room into a 4,000-pound box that fits into the backseat of your car.

I was waiting with just such a box on a hand truck near the exit, when my attention wandered for a moment. I saw out of the corner of my eye that the box was tipping off of the hand truck and was about to crash into a sliding-glass door. Without thinking, I lunged to catch it, barely snagging the corner of the box with my fingers in an awkward, fully extended position. The box didn't really weigh 4,000 pounds, but it was more weight than I could have managed even in perfect conditions. Naturally the box ripped through my fingers and flung me to the floor.

That night my back was in spasms, and I had shooting nerve pain in my right leg. After a few days it seemed to clear up, but every few years I would overextend something and end up in bed for a day, twitching.

Fast-forward to adulthood. I've got two kids and am too old to do things without limbering up first, so now the time between back-pain events has shortened. And one Saturday I woke up with it bad. I could barely breathe through the pain. We went the ER, where they gave me muscle relaxers, pain meds, and referred me to my primary care doctor.

Oh, wait. I don't have a primary care doctor because I don't ever go to the doctor. "Pick one, I guess," was my poorly chosen path forward. I was given an address with an appointment time, and I drove off.

Pulling up to what appeared to be an abandoned elementary school, I was certain I'd come to the wrong place. When I saw a police car parked outside the front door, I turned the car to drive off. Then I saw what looked to be a temporary plastic sign hanging down over the school name. It bore the logo of my medical network. I had arrived.

I knew that different people have different access to health care, but it had never occurred to me that the health care *experience* could be so different. As I waited in seemed to be the student commons, a worker saw me using my computer and came over. He was beside himself with excitement that someone was using his WiFi—it had been a struggle to get it approved, and I was apparently the first to use it.

The whole experience was a little surreal: The thin and very pregnant doctor with the slight Russian accent, harshly lit by the flickering fluorescent bulb. The coarse, skeptical X-ray tech, who assured me as he worked, "Man, this [expletive] ain't gonna do nothing. Okay, turn... You got nerve problems, man. Turn... X-rays don't show nothin' for nerve pain. Okay, turn... you're wastin' your time. All right, have a nice day."

I returned for one follow-up appointment and learned that the tech was right. I needed an MRI, not just X-rays. I mentioned that my pain medicine didn't seem to be helping, and the doctor told me, "Then you should stop taking it. We can't prescribe anything stronger, and you can still get addicted to it even if it's not working."

To this day, it's probably my favorite medical experience. Why? It took me a while to figure out, but I finally did. It was *real*. Everything that happened there, in terms of process and results, would have happened in any regular doctor's office. "Regular" in my context translates to mostly white, mostly middle-class. So what made it real? Nobody there was catering to my white privilege. Nobody was holding my hand, trying to comfort me by saying, "It'll probably be fine and things will be back to normal soon. Okay, hon?" None of that. It was: "Your back hurts? Yeah, life has problems sometimes. Here's yours." Down to earth.

It was refreshing, really.

Life Gets Real

What's all that got to do with Advent? Everything.

Much of American Christianity holds this odd ideal of everything needing to be squeaky clean Christian. We've got our own music. We even have our own movies. We get to be picky about how we worship. We may not have walled ourselves off from our surroundings, but we've certainly inflated a bubble. We do that thing where we act like we've got it all together—until it's all fallen apart. When non-Christians look at Christians, they often don't see the down-to-earth realities that would make us seem approachable. We appear to be either in great shape or in a recovery program. But what about everything in between?

Everything in between is where we've got to learn to live a down-to-earth lifestyle. If life were really as rosy as we like to paint it, we wouldn't need to look for Jesus at Advent. Yet our Scripture is full of real people dealing with real life. Why is it so hard for us to engage that or admit that it's where we live?

Joseph and Mary were faced with a difficult surprise, along with some down-to-earth realities that deeply complicated their lifestyle. Their faithfulness in dealing with it—publicly, even—give our Advent season meaning that we may have missed out on.

Going Deeper

Traveling Light

When we go on vacation, it often looks like we're trying to take it all with us. We overpack and overpack, then bring some extra chairs just in case, more books than we could read in a year, fourteen ways to access the Internet, and two chargers for each of them. Then we arrive and realize we still managed to forget something. I've taken weeklong road trips by motorcycle, and there's a kind of joy to be found in the simplicity of having only so much room on the bike to carry anything. If it doesn't fit, you can't bring it. Simple as that.

But I've never traveled as lightly as Jesus instructed the disciples to do when he sent them out in Luke 9:1-6. Take a moment to read it.

Ever done anything like *that*? Try going on vacation sometime with "no walking stick, no bag, no bread, no money, not even an extra shirt" (v. 3)!

Keep in mind that the disciples had serious and probably terrifying work to do. Remember, they didn't think of themselves as "the disciples." These guys still had fishermen's hearts. To suddenly be given the power to heal and charged with proclaiming an upside-down kingdom—well, it might have been nice to let them take a bag of Gummy Bears or something. Just a little treat for a job well done.

Jesus' minimalism was flinging them into an incredibly down-to-earth lifestyle—they weren't preaching the Kingdom from a position of entitlement or power, or with any visible markers of success. At the end of their sermons, they still needed to find dinner and a place to sleep for the night. How different does that sound from the gospel you and I preach, often using well-appointed A/V? Which gospel has more down-to-earth conviction—the one with lots of nice stuff, or the one someone follows even when they have nothing?

For reflection:

- When people look at you as a Christian, what lifestyle do they see? Someone who is Christian because of what goes with it, or someone who is Christian regardless of possessions or personal gain?
- Are there things you feel your faith entitles you to? What, and why?

Get Between the Toes, Please

In the US, we don't have to deal with dirty feet the way they do in lots of other cultures. We have more asphalt than dirt. Shoes are better than they used to be. All in all, people of average means stay pretty clean.

So it's difficult in a tangible way to process certain stories in Scripture. Looking at Luke 9:5, we can sort of resonate with Jesus' instructions to the disciples: "Wherever they don't welcome you, as you leave that city, shake the dust off your feet as a witness against them." After all, most of us have knocked mud or snow off our shoes before going inside or getting in a car. And it does sound like a sweet way to show disdain: "Fine; we won't even take your *dust* with us. Good day, sir. I said, Good *day,* sir." (Exit disciples in a huff.)

Now take a look at John 13:1-17, the story of Jesus washing the disciples' feet. The job of footwashing does sound gross, and the disciples' discomfort in the story was obvious. Today a lot of people are squeamish about even having their feet touched, let alone washed, but back then it happened all the time.

So what bothered the disciples? It was the idea of Jesus taking the role of a servant. Get that churchy "put others first" thing out of your head for a second and consider this: Jesus had taken the role of an *actual* servant—the underling who did those mundane-to-unpleasant tasks that regular people either wouldn't or just didn't do for themselves. The disciples were uncomfortable because Jesus was being the person in the room whom they had trained themselves to ignore.

The disciples learned two things in that moment: they probably were a little chagrined at how *normal* it felt to ignore servants, not really even viewing them as people; and, even more uncomfortably, they saw Jesus demonstrating that *this* was how they were to approach the world. Down-to-earth living. Right down to the actual dust of the earth.

For reflection:

- You probably don't have paid servants, but who are the service people in your life whom you tend to ignore? Gas station attendants, grocery store clerks—who are the everyday people you see but don't engage as people?
- If footwashing—an act of servanthood—is Jesus' example of a down-to-earth lifestyle, how are you following it?

My Neighbor?

You knew we were headed here eventually: the Great Commandment. Read Matthew 22:34-40.

In this passage, Jesus' response to the legal expert was, at once, a really good point, a mic drop, and a little bit of a magic trick. Throughout the Gospels, when Jesus was questioned by Pharisees or experts in the law, they tried to trap him in his words, get him to contradict himself, or in some way appear to go against the teachings of Scripture. It's hard in this example to tell if that's what the legal expert was doing or whethe.,r he was simply curious about Jesus' opinion. Jesus' answer though, was sensational: love God, love your neighbor.

The magic trick part is that in these two statements, Jesus summed up the *hundreds* of detailed laws contained in the Hebrew Scripture. If you do just these two simple things, he was saying, you satisfy all those hundreds of things.

Of course, neither statement is really that simple.

For reflection:

- What is your biggest struggle in loving God with everything you have? Where do you hold back?
- How do you find it hard to love your neighbor? Awkwardly for us, neighbor is an inclusive word—really, anybody who isn't your enemy is your neighbor, right? Oh, whoops, we're supposed to love our enemy, too. You mean we're supposed to love everybody?

Making It Personal

The biggest difficulty in living a genuinely down-to-earth lifestyle is that it comes with a loss of control. It admits that everything won't always be as we'd like it to be, and that's okay.

A couple of years ago, the A/C conked out at our house. This was a very disappointing development, as we have grown accustomed to personalized climate control over the years. There was an odd (and unreasonable) sense that we'd failed as people somehow—this central piece of American suburbia had broken, and we couldn't afford to fix it. What would the neighbors think?

The summer that followed ended up being a great reminder of the realities of a down-to-earth lifestyle. You can't control everything. Not every part of your life is going to be the same temperature. There may be parts of the day where it's better not to be in the house. Oh, and it's okay to sweat a little.

I'm glad to have that sense of control back—we were able to replace our system right before winter—but I remain grateful for the reminder. When you look at your own life, are there places where your lifestyle is separating you from the realities experienced by others?

Sharing Thoughts and Feelings

Spend some time with a group discussing these questions:

- What does it mean to you to live a down-to-earth lifestyle? Are there parts of that idea that appeal to you? Are there parts that don't?
- When it comes to Advent, where do you see a down-to-earth lifestyle being lived out in the stories we share from Scripture this time of year?
- In what ways does your current lifestyle separate you from the lifestyle being lived by others? What's good or bad in that?
- How does your church demonstrate down-to-earth-ness in your community?
- What are some ways you can more fully embrace the idea of allowing your community's reality into your life?

Doing Things Together

Servant

Supplies: A large bowl of water, a towel

Footwashing as a spiritual exercise has had some popularity over the years. Sometimes it's done in a small group or retreat setting. There are summer mission organizations that end their week with a big group footwashing, suggesting ways in which the group can serve each other, just as they've been serving others outside of their group all week.

I don't love the footwashing practice. I'm not a big fan of forced intimacy, and in fact any kind of you-must-touch-each-other in youth ministry always was a red flag for me. I feel that footwashing often pushes people out of their comfort zones more than it teaches any kind of servant's attitude. (I've also found that getting "out of our comfort zones" as a virtue is just another way of telling people what to do and having them comply. But I digress.)

Ask: Was anyone instantly uncomfortable just looking at the bowl of water and the towel? What emotions did you feel when you saw them?

The reason I'd argue that footwashing doesn't really teach a servant's attitude is that we don't have this particular role of servant in our current culture. I mean, sure, it makes the washer do a potentially gross thing on behalf of the other person. But it also forces the washer into a position of vulnerability, which to me doesn't sound like putting the other person first.

So, since most of us don't need our feet washed most of the time, what's an *actual* need in our current culture that would demonstrate a servant's attitude? Brainstorm something your small group could do together that represents a servant's heart and meets an actual need in today's world. Offer to do someone's laundry. Cut their grass. Wash their car. Pick up groceries for them. It's up to you!

Break the Bubble

Supplies: paper and pens

- Divide your small group into two teams. Each team is to pick a popular sport and come up with the *Christian* rules for that sport. The sport will remain basically the same, but you can play with some new rules for playing and scoring, or even some new objectives. How would you play Christian basketball? Christian baseball? Don't do dodgeball; some would argue that we've perfected Christian dodgeball already.

After discussing it in small groups, have your large group gather and share what they came up with. Listeners can push back at presenters if they disagree. When both teams have shared, ask:

- Why do we have Christian versions of some things and not others? Why do we have Christian books and movies but not Christian sports?
- Most of the things we've Christianized fall into the category of the arts, which is interesting because, in theory, the arts are where we express our most real selves. What does it say to non-Christian artists that we pull away from their creations and culturally isolate ourselves?
- During Advent, we recognize that Jesus came modeling a disruptive, down-to-earth lifestyle. The early church didn't withdraw from culture, it permeated it. What are some reasons why we aren't more like that today?

Listening for God

God, thank you for sending, in Jesus, such a beautiful picture of down-to-earth living. May we find new ways to follow in his footsteps every day. Amen!

4.

Down to Earth
Obedience

4.

DOWN TO EARTH OBEDIENCE

*Therefore, my loved ones, just as you always obey me,
not just when I am present but now even more while I
am away, carry out your own salvation with fear and
trembling. God is the one who enables you both to want
and to actually live out his good purposes.*

(Philippians 2:12-13)

Reading and Reflecting

Dressed for Success

I've been threatening my children for *weeks* about what stories might
end up in this chapter. I said, "Go to sleep! Don't make me write about
you in the obedience chapter." We'll see how it works out for them.

When it came down to choosing a primary story to express down-to-earth obedience, I decided to go with one from my own childhood. I honestly don't remember how old I was, but my older brother and I got to go on one of those week-long youth summer camps. This wasn't one that runs all summer and you pick which week you want to go—it was more of an event. Fun and games all day, worship with a band every night. It wasn't our first extended stay away from home, but it was our first like this. We spent a whole afternoon picking out T-shirts and shorts for the daytime activities and nicer Sunday clothes for the evening worship services.

If you've ever been to a week-long summer youth event, your ears may have perked up at that last bit. I don't remember what the brochure said specifically, but my mom understood it to mean that we were meant to show up dressed for Easter every evening. It was probably something like "casual attire for worship," which I can imagine my mom understood as "not what you've been wearing all day." Stay tuned.

The Big Time

So, we got dropped off at whatever college was hosting us. As a pre-teen, these kinds of away-from-home experiences feel like you've hit the big time, and I was eating it up. You meet new kids, make new friends, and have a fresh shot at sizing yourself up against your peers in terms of height, weight, speed, agility, coolness, style…basically all the stuff we said not to do in the humility chapter.

My big moment to shine was on the volleyball court, where I ended up in a game with kids at least two grades above me. I was dwarfed in height, but for some reason that day the ability to play volleyball was on me like stink: I served a full-game shutout. I know it sounds unbelievable, because it happened to me and *I* can barely believe it. For an afternoon, I was a hero. The rest of the week I declined invitations to play volleyball, certain that the truth about my ability would be exposed.

That night at dinner, my brother and I got our first hint that we may have overpacked. Somebody suggested going to the outdoor basketball court after we finished eating. One of asked, "If we play basketball, how will we have time to change before worship?"

"Change?" came the quick reply. Gulp.

Declining the hoops invite, my brother and I reconvened in the dorm room. It was now obvious that *no one else* had any intention of changing before worship. Worse, it was pretty clear that no one running the camp *expected* any of us to show up looking like anything but campers. All the adults were still in T-shirts and shorts, too. Ugh.

Our problem? Mom had said to wear the church clothes—no ifs, ands, or buts. The overwhelming reality that Mom had misunderstood the dress code had no bearing on the situation. Our mom, not reachable for comment, had given us instructions. (This was in the days before cell phones.) My status as volleyball hero was about to be stomped out by a pair of dress shoes.

We quickly reviewed our options. (A) We could stick with our T-shirts and shorts, knowing that our mom would totally (hopefully) understand that everyone else had done the same. (B) One of us could do what our mom had told us, while the other rolled the dice by ignoring it. This option was tricky, because it set up one of us to be destroyed if we were wrong, or to get told on, which was more likely.

You guessed it: We went with (C), in which two of the finest dressed boys you ever did see went tromping down to worship, eyes fixed on the ground. This didn't turn into a not-as-bad-as-we-thought scenario; it was hell. We saw disbelief in the faces of the friends we'd already made, and outright laughter from high school girls. You could tell they thought we were cute, but it was the pathetic kind of cute. Oh, there were *so many* nights of worship that week.

I think after the first night we conceded that we could ditch the dress shoes. Other than that, every night after dinner we sucked it up and got our button-down selves to worship.

Without Question

Now *that*, my friends, is down-to-earth obedience.

You should know, most moms have eyes in the back of their heads, but our mom had eyes in the back of her soul. Geographic separation provided no quarter from Mom's ability to spot misbehavior. This, in a way, was the kind of obedience Paul was talking about in his letter to the Philippians: "Therefore, my loved ones, just as you always obey me, not just when I am present but now even more while I am away . . ." (v. 12). Paul was inviting the Philippians to continue moving forward in their spirituality and practice even when he wasn't there to guide them.

In a way, we experience that opportunity every time we leave our church environment and head out into the world. It's an obvious mistake to leave behind all that we've learned and shared in church; after all, what's the point in learning to be a Christian if we do that?

Here in Advent, we are invited to experience and show down-to-earth obedience. Jesus is coming into the world for a season—to show us the way, to provide an example, to step into the room for a moment, bringing his good news.

Our very lives are an invitation to join in that way, to be obedient to that call. It won't always be fun. There's no promise that your volleyball rock-star status will hold up. But if we're serious about becoming part of an upside-down kingdom, there's no point in being at the top. Obedience isn't about you. It's about all of us.

Going Deeper

One Time

Okay, I thought I was going to let my sons off the hook, but this passage is too perfect to leave them out any longer. Read Jesus' parable of two sons, Matthew 21:28-31a.

My older son (sorry about this, Grey) suffers from a condition known as *brushticular disinclination*, which is a diagnosable but untreatable aversion to brushing one's teeth. Research shows that symptoms fade with age. There's a cream, but I'd rather not get into that, so we're back at square one. We've discovered a trigger phrase that causes a flare-up in his symptoms: any adult saying, "Grey, brush your teeth."

He moves when you tell him, even saying, "Yes, sir," but he's moving to do anything *but* brush his teeth. If we go back a few minutes later and ask what he's been doing, he'll say things such as, "Going to the bathroom," "Picking out my clothes," "Nothing" (that's a favorite of ours), or any number of other activities that aren't toothbrush-related. I recently caught myself saying, "*One time*, Grey. One time I'd love to say, 'Brush your teeth,' and have brushing be the next thing that happens."

Then there's Penner, Grey's younger brother. Penner is prone not to respond at all and simply do the thing we asked him to. I'll call into the next room, "Penner, brush your teeth," which will be followed by several minutes of silence. A little louder I'll say, "*Penner*. What are you *doing*?"

"MMMMMBUSHUNG MMMMMTEEEEEF!" Oh. Brushing your teeth. How was I supposed to know if you didn't answer me?

And so I ask you: Which son obeyed?

Grey starts middle school next year, and he would like you to know that he's tall, good-looking, and excited about dismantling Steph Curry's middle-school basketball stats. (Grey hasn't read Chapter 2.)

In seriousness, my story of the two sons shows there are at least two ways to show our obedience to God: in what we say and in what we do. In Jesus' version of the story, you could argue that *neither* son obeyed.

One had an attitude problem. The other had an action problem.

For reflection:

- Which do you struggle with more, wanting to obey or actually obeying? Which do you struggle with in relation to God's call on your life?
- How do you show others that you're living in obedience? Is that important to you?

The Voice in Your Ear

Read John 14:15-26.

The good news is that if we're obedient, our instructions come with tech support! It would have been awesome that week at camp if we'd been able just to *ask* Mom if we could go to worship in our T-shirts. Since we couldn't ask her, we were forced to stick with the last instructions received. For the record, we scored huge bonus points for that when we got home. I think our parents were more than a little surprised that we had complied in the face of such enormous peer pressure. Honestly, I remain surprised as well.

Jesus must have seen the advantages of having someone to ask, because in John 14:26 he lets his followers know they won't be completely on their own: "The Companion, the Holy Spirit, whom the Father will send in my name, will teach you everything and will remind you of everything I told you."

Wouldn't it make things easier if we had God's voice right in our ear, telling us what to do and reminding us of what Jesus said? Oh, wait. We do! The Holy Spirit remains here with us still, speaking into our lives—if we'll just listen. So, how do we listen?

We've got options. We've got a more complete understanding of God through our Scripture. We have each other. And we really do have the Holy Spirit, speaking to us directly, through other believers, and through the Bible.

For reflection:

- How do you listen for God's voice in your life?
- How can others hear the Spirit's word through you?
- How has pursuing God helped you remain obedient to God?

Love Your Enemies

When Jesus says you should love your enemies, it's not just because it sounds like the most Christian thing to do. Jesus says to love your enemies because Jesus wants you to love your enemies.

Read Luke 6:27-36.

This is the upside-down kingdom, remember? The key to being a part of it is learning to do the most loving thing imaginable in any and every situation. This practice especially kicks in when you are faced with a situation in which anger or negativity is expected or maybe even justified, according to the way we're accustomed to thinking. Jesus rolls through some pretty common slights and offers simple but difficult responses: Love your enemies. Bless those who curse you. Don't meet violence with violence. Give more than people try to take from you. Treat people the way you'd like to be treated, even if that's not how they're treating you— *especially* if that's not how they're treating you.

I find verse 35 especially striking: "You will be acting the way children of the Most High act, for he is kind to ungrateful and wicked people." This isn't just advice—it's an opportunity for down-to-earth obedience. This is how God behaves; if you want to be a part of the kingdom, be like that.

Thank God we've been sent a Companion! We're going to need reminding.

For reflection:

- What situations or people test your ability to act "the way children of the Most High act"?
- Are there situations in which you're good at loving and serving your enemies?
- How do you balance the people you call enemies and the people you call neighbors? What's the difference if we're meant to love both?

Making It Personal

Obedience to anything external is difficult at times.

When I moved out of the local church youth ministry into full-time freelance writing a couple of years ago, I felt this enormous freedom— now *nobody* can tell me what to do! I get to choose who I work with and what I work on! It's great to be me!

All that is true, but as the year progressed I realized that I've *always* had that freedom; I just hadn't recognized it. I was always able to choose where I worked, how I would respond in various situations, and to whom I would give mental energy. If I ever felt trapped in my work, I was ignoring the fact that I had made the decision to be there.

Choosing to walk in obedient step with Jesus is like that—you're making a decision about who you'd like to follow, who you'd like to model your life after, even who you might be willing to sacrifice your life for someday. As we prepare during Advent for the coming of Jesus, we're reminded continually of the example he's given us by his own dedication to living in obedience before God. When seen in that way, obedience isn't a chore; obedience is the natural outflow of a commitment.

You may not be ready yet to make that commitment. If you're aware that you aren't, it's perfectly cool. It shows that you grasp the dedication required as part of that commitment and that it's not to be made lightly. Take some time this week to talk with a parent or church leader about where you are personally in the process of deciding what obedience to God might look like in your life.

Sharing Thoughts and Feelings

Spend some time with a group discussing these questions:

- Last down-to-earth definition: What does "down-to-earth obedience" mean to you?
- What was a time when you had the most difficulty being obedient?

- When have you been intentionally disobedient? How did that work out for you?
- What is involved in obedience to God? Is it just following a bunch of rules, or is it more active than that?
- How does God usually get your attention when you need reminding about something?

Doing Things Together

Do It, Do It Now

- Play the classic children's game *Simon Says*, with this variation: have *two* leaders.
- The ordinary game play goes like this: Whoever is Simon (or Simone) offers simple instructions, such as "Simon says pat your tummy." Each time the instruction begins with the words, "Simon says," it must be followed. If the instruction does *not* begin with "Simon says," it must *not* be followed. Simon/Simone's goal is to call out instructions rapidly enough that, in confusion, someone will follow a command that didn't start with "Simon says." With *two* leaders going at the same time, it will be even more confusing.

Should you focus on a single leader or try to follow both at the same time? That's for you to decide! Best of luck.

Play the game to a winner. If you have time to repeat it, you can clarify any rules you'd like to change, but do keep two leaders in play. Afterward, debrief with the following questions:

- What was challenging about playing this version of Simon Says?
- What did you like about it? What did you not like?
- When you're faced in life with two or more possible ways to handle a situation, how do you determine the best way forward?

- Describe a time when you've had difficulty obeying leadership in your life. How did you handle it?
- Do you think it's freeing or confining to have someone guide you?
- When do you struggle to obey someone? Do you ever find other voices distracting you from God? What are they?

... And Repeat

- More *Simon Says*! This time, instead of one or even two leaders trying to trick the group into following the wrong command, you'll each take turns being the leader for a single command. Your goal this time, though, is to give commands that are *extremely* difficult to follow. Try to make it possible to follow the commands, but a real challenge. Here are a few examples if you need them:
- Simon says to stand in a deep knee-bend on one foot for a full minute.
- Simon says to scream longer than anyone in the room.
- Simon says to hold your breath for a minute and thirty seconds.

You get the idea. Challenging, but possible. Keep going until everyone has had a turn or two (or three!). Then wrap up with these questions:

- How do you feel when you're asked to do something that stretches you beyond your ordinary capabilities, not just in the game we played but in real life? What emotions do you experience when you realize that obedience may involve failure?
- When have you chosen not to obey someone because you feared failure? What was the result?
- What aspects of your faith do you find the most challenging as you try to obey God?
- How do you find strength to live into a down-to-earth obedience to God?

Listening for God

God, during Advent we are so grateful that you came to us in Jesus, as a perfect example of down-to-earth love, humility, lifestyle, and obedience. Give us strength to imitate him. Give us resolve. Help us to remember that we have community with others who are on the same journey here at church! Show us where we can provide support to others when they struggle, and help us be willing to accept support from others.

Your love is all we need. Thank you for the great gift of love that we're preparing to receive at Christmas. May we carry that love with us through the entire year. We praise and love you. Amen!